There Was an Old Man with a Springbok

The author wishes to thank the editors of the following magazines: *Ampersand Review, The Awl, Best American Poetry* website, *B O D Y, Boston Review, Buenos Aires Review* (Argentina), *Fanzine, Fjords, Kettle Blue Review, Little Star, NONSITE, Paris Review Daily, Poetry, A Poetry Congeries, Prelude, Puerto del Sol, Riddle Fence* (Canada), *Sprung Formal, TAG, T A G VV E R K, Tammy, TUBA, Underwater New York, Vice*.

The Prelude Press LLC
PO Box 110593
Brooklyn, NY 11211

Stu Watson and Robert C.L. Crawford, Publishers

Illustrated by Mark Fletcher
Designed by Mike Newton

preludebooks.com
preludemag.com

ISBN 978-0-9907030-8-2

There Was an Old Man with a Springbok

Anthony Madrid

Illustrated by Mark Fletcher

PRELUDE

There was an old man with a springbok,
Who said "I just can't feel a thing, Doc.
This gazelle on my neck has a numbing effect."
So the doctor examined the springbok.

There was an old priest from the Point,
Who had to sit down to anoint.
His ankle was sore, ’cuz an ankylosaur
Irrepressibly gnawed at the joint.

There was a young man from the Bronx,
Who loved drawing and redrawing ankhs.
When they asked for specifics, he spoke hieroglyphics,
That vexing young man from the Bronx.

There was an old man at the auction,
Who was sipping a homemade concoction.
It caused him to bid on a caryatid,
Which he carried about at the auction.

There was an old person whose zeal
Made him bug-eyed and tense at the wheel.
He wasn’t much fun, and they said he was un-
representative of their ideal.

We saw some young mothers from Chatham,
Whose children were looking right at ’em.
“You children are buggin’ us! Quit standing there huggin’ us!”
Said those grumpy young mothers from Chatham.

There was a young man from Glen Burnie,
Who, in trying to find an attorney,
Went to lawyers.com, and then phoned up his mom,
And said “Mom! I have found an attorney!”

There was a small party from Brooklyn,
Who, wherever their destiny took them,
Would establish a base and get up in your face,
And remind you of why you left Brooklyn.

There was an old lady from Bozeman,
Who greatly resembled a clothespin.
The part in her hair was remarkably square,
So her husband inserted his nose in.

There was an old person from Skokie,
Who had spent a few years in the pokey.
His facial tattoos never failed to amuse
The municipal workers of Skokie.

There was an old man from Oak Lawn,
Who said "But the show must go on!"
When they got him arrested, he gently protested:
"OK! But the show must go on!"

There was an old man from New Trier,
Who decided to brew up some beer.
When they said "Is it brewing?" he said "Nothing doing!"
That petulant man from New Trier.

There was an old man from Madrid,
Whose poetry went off the grid.
He longed to recite, and yet somehow in spite
Of that sumptuous fact, never did.

There was an old person whose property
Compelled him to take up topography.
When they told him to stop, he replied like a fop:
"I should know the extent of my property!"

There was a young man from Waukegan,
Who was happily dating a vegan.
There were times when he irked her by eating a burger,
But each found the other intriguing.

There was an old man from Hyde Park,
Whose prediction was wide of the mark.
What he thought was a kitten turned out to have bitten
His hand with the force of a shark.

There was an old man of Vancouver,
Who, in shopping, knew how to maneuver.
When they said "Whatcha doin'?" he said "I'm canoeing!"
That beautiful man of Vancouver.

There was an old person from Edgewater,
Who sáid "Back away from the ledge, Daughter."
But she threatened to jump, and engendered a lump
In the throat of that person from Edgewater.

There was an old man from Sichuan,
Who directed the kids on his lawn.
He was rather aloof, and would sit on the roof,
And descend only when they had gone.

There was an old person from Melbourne,
Who neglected to silence his cell phone.
A disturbance arose when he tore off his clothes
In attempting to silence that cell phone.

There was an old man from El Paso,
Whose rodeo stunt was to lasso
A gazelle and a buck, load 'em into a truck,
And then pass through the tolls of El Paso.

There was an old man at O'Hare,
Whose behavior was cause of despair.
He tried to get into the overhead bin,
'Cuz he thought that that thing was his chair.

There was an old man at the Strand,
Whose focaccia got way out of hand.
It exploded with crumbs, and now nobody comes
Within five hundred feet of the Strand.

There was a young girl from Ohio,
Who contracted acute impetigo.
This staphylococcal outrageous debacle
Disturbed that young girl from Ohio.

There was an old man from Kenosha:
You never saw anything gaucher!
His hair was a frizz | and, not only that, his
Manischewitz was not even kosher.

There was an old person whose wiener
Turned green, and then it turned greener.
When he went to the doctor, he thoroughly shocked her,
That gruesome old man with a wiener.

There was an old person from Burnside,
And his garden was good 'til his fern died.
He threw it a funeral, and said "Play a tune, or I'll
Sink in despair, since my fern died."

There was an old man from Connecticut,
Who couldn't tell subject from predicate.
His sense of declension was cause of some tension
To people who lived in Connecticut.

There was an old person from Lawndale,
First cousin to Senator Mondale.
She voted for Carter, but said it was harder
To jump up and down about Mondale.

There was a young mother from Chelsea,
Whose children were not at all healthy.
When they wanted a cuddle, they'd squirt out a puddle,
Which troubled the people of Chelsea.

There was an old man from DuPage,
Whom we had to confine to a cage.
His shoes and his pants were imported from France,
But he tore them apart in a rage.

There was an old man from Three Forks:
All three of his children were dorks.
They went on safari, but said "We are sorry,
But we have to go back to Three Forks!"

There was an old man from Messina,
Who perceived he'd been served a subpoena.
When he went to his lawyer, he greatly annoyed her
By whining about the subpoena.

There was an old person from Oak Brook,
Who took dówn all we said in a notebook.
When we asked to revise it, he didn't advise it,
And wouldn't let go of the notebook.

There was a young girl from Missoula,
Who was greatly in need of a doula.
Her baby was crowning, which seemed quite astounding
To folks on the bus from Missoula.

There was a young girl named McDonough,
Who said "Nó one can stop me, I'm gonna."
She proceeded to swallow some tikka masala:
A barrel! a mountain! a ton o'!

There was an old person from Tucson,
Who refused to keep both of his shoes on.
With regard to his gloves, it's the same as above,
And was spoken-of all over Tucson.

There was an old man on Pulaski,
Who tried to get in with a pass key.
When it broke in the lock, he proceeded to knock
On the doors of that block of Pulaski.

There was a balloonist from Madison,
Who refused, when we told him to jettison.
He got dówn in his basket, and said "If you ask it
Again, I will spit up my medicine."

There was an old man with a wombat,
Whose addiction to physical combat
Was partially hampered when somebody tampered
With half their equipment for combat.

There was a young lady whose fluff puff
I simply could not get enough of.
I shall never know what | put the spell on me, but
I could not get enough of her fluff puff!

There was an old man at the Louvre,
Holding on by one hand from the roof.
When they said "Should we catch ya?" he answered "You betcha!"
But wouldn't let go of the roof.

There was a young person named Wheeler,
Preserved in a jar of tequila.
"I'm a gnat! I'm a gnat!" was the comment of that
Hymenopterous person named Wheeler.

There was an old person from Niles,
Whose resistance to feminine wiles
Was a proverb among | the infirm and the young
And the people who meet with such trials.

There was a young lady at Taco Bell,
Whose toppings were those of an infidel.
Her beef enchilada was cause of a lotta
Distress to the people at Taco Bell.

There was an old person from Maine,
Who loved to sing songs in the rain.
He sang *a cappella* but broke his umbrella,
And everyone said "What a shame!"

There was a young girl from Virginia
—I hesitate now to continue—
No matter in bed, she would lecture you dead
On the Dharma without and within ya.

There was an old person from Portland,
Who didn't think it was important
To put on a belt, 'cuz he said that he felt
He would only be walking 'round Portland.

There was an old person named Fletcher,
Who was carried away on a stretcher.
When he said "Put me down," they one-eightied around,
And then brought him back home on the stretcher.

There was an old person from Lisle,
Who had us all beat by a mile.
When we said "What's your secret?" he slowly proceeded
To read us a treatise on style.

There was an old man from Lemont,
Who said "What the fuck do they want?
I am only a slime, but they act as if I'm
As astute as Immanuel Kant."

There was a young lady from Ottawa,
Who thought she was Anna Akhmatova.
Her relentless hauteur made her friends insecure,
But she didn't care what people thoughtovva.

There was a young girl from Xinjiang,
With whom we could not get along.
Her suspenders were girdles; her tortoises, turtles;
Her sandals were thirty feet long.

There was a young man from St James,
Who consigned all his work to the flames.
When asked why he did it, he sadly admitted
It's one of his dumb little games.

There was an old lady from Shiloh,
Who rode up to town on a rhino.
When they laughed her to scorn, she would lean on the horn,
And then parallel park on a wino.

I've had 'bout enough of your nutmeg.
I wanna stand up, but on *what* leg?
When I tried to get cinnamon, most of the women in
Line said they only had nutmeg.

There was a young man on the driveway,
Who tried to put wheels on his Steinway.
He concocted a plan to play Bach and Chopin
While they wheeled him around on the driveway.

There was an old person from Naperville,
Who was second to none at the paper mill.
He could oil the machine and then whip up a ream
With the speed of a gun or a power drill.

There was an old person whose flatulence
Shook the kitchen right down to its spatulas.
The ladles and strainers and pasta containers
Were SMASHED on account of that flatulence.

There was an old man from Las Cruces,
Who, no mátter what ány of yóu says,
Was pensive and kind, and was seldom inclined
To indulge in medieval abuses.

There was an old person from Elmhurst,
Who said "Nóbody else in this realm durst
Make show of their force, with exception of course
Of myself, who am Warlord of Elmhurst."

There was an old man from Bay Ridge,
Who was deathly afraid of the fridge.
But he bought a pet pigeon and changed his religion
And now they both pray to the fridge.

We saw a few artists from Bensonhurst,
But I'm nót sure which one I should mention first.
This one guy we saw was unwilling to draw,
'Cuz he wanted to sharpen his pencil first.

There was a young girl from McLean,
Who was caught with a gun on the plane.
The Captain attacked, but he had to go back,
Because no one was flying the plane.

There was an old person from Pilsen,
Who was peacefully smoking until some-
one turned up the gas, which exploded, alas,
Leaving wreckage of what had been Pilsen.

There was an old lawyer whose peppermints
Could not be allowed into Evidence.
His bagel and cereal were ruled immaterial,
In light of Procedure and Precedents.

There was a young girl from Annapolis,
Whose apples were totally fabulous.
Her bananas were precious and greatly impressed us
As better than most in Annapolis.

There was a small party from Gresham,
No amount of iced tea would refresh 'em.
So we read 'em some verse, and they said "Now it's worse,
And indeed we don't need this aggression."

There was an old person from Edmonton:
A deliciously ladylike gentleman.
The goalies and centers approved his suspenders:—
They'd never seen any more feminine.

There was an old man from the Ozarks,
Who was constantly pestered by loan sharks.
They chased him around but eventually found
He had tunneled up under the Ozarks.

The way she ate lunch on a bicycle
Could not be considered advisable,—
For potatoes au gratin were constantly caught in
The spokes of the wheels of her bicycle.

There was an old man from Canarsie,
Who wrote all his poems in Farsi.
"Yes, but how 'bout a version without all this Persian?"
Complained all the kids at Canarsie.

There was a mortician from Havre,
Who successfully washed a cadaver.
When they said "That's your talent," he answered "I doubt it,"
That roundabout person from Havre.

There was an old man on Paulina:
You never saw anything finer!
His hat was so big that he | channeled the dignity
Of Beethoven's Mass in B-minor.

There was an old person of Minsk,
Who, despite all we said, was convinced
That the easiest way to unload all that hay
Was to call for assistance from Minsk.

There was an old person from Dallas,
Whose comportment was colored by malice.
When we tried to take naps, he would sit in our laps,
And complain of a pain in his phallus.

There was an old man who would bite-cha.
We called him a jerk and said "Whyncha
Go chew on yourself, you annoying old elf!"
But he'd bite-cha again just to spite-cha.

There was an old man from Park Slope,
Who was strangely unable to cope.
When we called in the medics, they said his genetics
Suggested there wasn't much hope.

There was an old man from Seattle:
Four fifths of his life was a battle.
He argued and fought, but eventually thought:
"It is time to desist from the battle."

There was an old person from Sauganash,
Who was constantly sucking back succotash.
Until he repented, he gave us incentive
To battle our way out of Sauganash.

There was an old man from Fort Greene,
Who was urged by the cops to come clean.
They nevertheless wouldn't let him confess
'Cuz they saw they were just being mean.

There was a young man from the Netherlands,
Who could hardly contain his malevolence.
Always losing his head, until somebody said:
"It is time you went back to the Netherlands."

There was an old person from Reno,
Who decided to eat a neutrino.
He spoke in Hawaiian, and looked like that guy in
That painting by Parmigianino.

There was an old man with a dik-dik,
Who depicted himself in a triptych.
In the first of the panels, he had on his flannels,
And animals handing him lipstick.

We saw a few folks from Chicago,
But all that they brought was a taco.
So they went to get pizza, and lost all their seats at the
Lollapalooza palazzo.

There was an old couple whose plumber
Thought their plumbing was kind of a bummer.
Both their toilet and tub were horrendously plugged,
And had been that way most of the summer.

There was an old man at DePaul:
Made disturbances down at the mall.
His beret was so tight that it made him turn white,
And they said "Why'dja *buy* it so small?"

There was a young lady named Hong,
Who delighted the world with her song.
She tore off her coat, and embarked on a note
Which she did all she could to prolong.

There was an old person from Bucktown,
Who was filling his pillow with duck down.
So he snatched up a wad, and then, using a rod,
Started priming that pillow with duck down.

There was an old man from Dekalb:
The washer was shot on his valve.
So it dribbled and dripped 'til his patience was stripped
And he sat around stupid and growled.

There was an old person from Evanston,—
And he certainly wasn't a pleasant one.
When we said "What's your deal?" he replied "I just feel
That you people are boring and meddlesome."

There was an old person from Billings:
When he laughed, you could see half his fillings.
He would snap at a moth, and his hat would fall off,
And they'd have to come get him from Billings.

There was an old man from Salinas,
Who tried to sign checks with his penis.
When we told him to quit it, he sat down and knitted
Some booties and hats for his penis.

There was an old person from Douglas,
Was in need of a hug but was hug-less.
When he got up and fled, we pursued him and said
"Let us *hug* you, Old Person from Douglas!"

There was an old person from Flint,
Who was partially covered in lint.
When we said "Why are you like this?" he got so self-righteous
We thought he would never relent.

There was an old man from LeSage,
Who was making a Bible collage!
But he needed a scissor, 'cuz Nebuchadnezzar
Looked more like the Wizard of Oz.

That basement has always depressed us,
On account of it's full of asbestos.
Said Governor Rauner: "I wouldn't go down there
Unless you're all into asbestos."

There was an old man with a backpack:
No body could beat him at blackjack.
When they said "Let us win!" he would finger his chin,
And then beat 'em to pieces at blackjack.

Both husband and wife on dialysis:
They picked apples until they had calluses.
They went to the orchard and happily tortured
Each other with brilliant analysis.

Distribution was strange in old Albuquerque:
One bath cap per duck, and one towelperturkey.
I certainly hope that each swan got a soap,
But you never can tell with old Albuquerque.

APPENDIX: FOUR FED-UP LIMERICKS

There was an old person from Habermas,
And his slobbering boss was a slobberboss.
And his bobbing with buoys, and gobbing with gooeys,
And all accusations of sabotage!

There was an old person from Fuckface,
Who greatly resembled a crankcase.
Such a stick-in-the-mud pulled the pin on the dud
And then ran up the wanks of the bank base!

There was an old person from Aardvark,
Who tried to skip over the hard part.
The concert promoter permitted an odor
That nobody voted for guard bark!

There was an old person whose shtwengpoppa
Responded "I can't feel a THING haha."
When we gave him a present, he said "Well it doesn't
Responded I can't feel a THING haha."

Anthony Madrid is the author of two other poetry books: *I Am Your Slave Now Do What I Say* (Canarium, 2012) and *Try Never* (Canarium, 2017). He lives in Victoria, Texas, with Nadya Pittendrigh.

Mark Fletcher is an illustrator and cartoonist. His work has been published in *Boston Review*, *Paris Review*, *B O D Y* and *Poetry*. Mark earned his BFA and BA in Art History from the University of Colorado. He lives in Colorado Springs, Colorado.

NOTES

Some of these limericks have owners. Suzanne Buffam, Jennifer Eldridge, Emily Kendal Frey, William Fuller, Rami Gabriel, Niko Georgiopoulos, Michael Hollander, Cathy Park Hong, Sandra Macpherson, Marie McDonough, Michael Robbins, Susan Wheeler, Gabe Winer. The "couple whose plumber" are the ones on dialysis, later. I know the *Mass in B-minor* is Bach.